Welcome to the Way!

A CONFIRMATION CATECHESIS

JUNIOR HIGH SCHOOL EDITION

Jim Bitney

Yvette Nelson

General Editors

Allen, Texas

Acknowledgments

Cover
Marshall Berman

Illustrations
Pages
  8 Christa Kieffer
10 Michel Allaire
14 Kathy Bottorff
18 Heather Preston
22 Kathy Bottorff
26 Heather Preston
30 Kathy Bottorff
38 Kathy Bottorff
42 Sandra Speidel
46 Kathy Bottorff
70 Sandra Speidel

Calligraphy
Georgia Deaver

Photographs
Pages
  4 Tony Arruza/Bruce Coleman
  5 © Bob Daemmrich
  6 Scala/Art Resource, NY: Mosaic (detail), Calling of Ss. Peter and Andrew, Ravenna, S. Apollinaire Nuovo.
  7 © Nick Pavloff
11 © Nick Pavloff
13 © Nita Winter
16 © David Frazier/The Stock Solution
17 © Marshall Berman
18 © Craig Aurness/West Light
20 © James L. Shaffer
21 © Bob Daemmrich
24 Lisa Means
27 © Jim Zuckerman/West Light
28 © Bob Daemmrich
29 Tony Arruza/Bruce Coleman
32 Lisa Means
35 © Bill Ross/West Light
36 © Bob Daemmrich

40 Lisa Means
43 © Nick Pavloff
44 © Nick Pavloff
49 © Jim Brandenburg/West Light
64 © James L. Shaffer
65 © James L. Shaffer
66 © James L. Shaffer
68 © Nick Pavloff
69 Norman Owen Tomalin/Bruce Coleman
71 © Willie Hill, Jr./The Image Works
72 © Nick Pavloff
73 © Bob Daemmrich
74 © Allen Russell/Profiles West
75 Scala/Art Resource, NY: El Greco, S. Pietro, Escorial, Spain.
76 Scala/Art Resource, NY: Michelangelo, Moses, S. Pietor in Vincoli.
77 © Nick Pavloff

Nihil Obstat:
Rev. Msgr. Mark Dosh
Censor Librorum

Imprimatur
† John R. Roach
Archbishop of Saint Paul and Minneapolis
April 2, 1989

Copyright © 1989 by Tabor Publishing,
a division of RCL Enterprises, Inc.

All rights reserved. No part of this book shall be reproduced or transmitted in any form or by any means, electronic or mechanical, including photocopying, recording, or by any information or retrieval system, without written permission from the Publisher.

Send all inquiries to:
Tabor Publishing
200 East Bethany Drive
Allen, Texas 75002-3804

Printed in the United States of America

ISBN 0-89505-585-6 (Student Text)

ISBN 0-89505-581-3 (Catechist's Edition)

ISBN 0-89505-583-X (Parish Manual)

6 7 8 9 10   98 97 96 95

CONTENTS

The Invitation	4
The Discovery	6
1 CHRIST	8
Close to Home	8
News of a Messiah	10
Becoming Church	12
Changing Things	14
Celebrating Christ	15
Discovery Journal	15
2 SPIRIT	16
People of Spirit	16
The Gift	18
Spirit Power	20
Surprised by the Spirit	22
Celebrating the Spirit	23
Discovery Journal	23
3 MISSION	24
Angel's Journey	24
Go for It!	26
Peace Is with You	28
Catching Fire	30
Celebrating Mission	31
Discovery Journal	31
4 CHURCH	32
Testing the Waters	32
A Day of Wind and Fire	34
Not by Yourself	36
Take a Stand—Together	38
Celebrating Church	39
Discovery Journal	39
5 MINISTRY	40
Just Be You!	40
Gifted for Ministry	42
Here to Help	44
We Need You	46
Celebrating Ministry	47
Discovery Journal	47
The Quest	48
1 WISDOM	50
2 UNDERSTANDING	52
3 JUDGMENT	54
4 COURAGE	56
5 KNOWLEDGE	58
6 REVERENCE	60
7 WONDER AND AWE	62
The Rite	64
CONFIRMED IN THE SPIRIT	66
The Treasury	68
1 A Sense of HOLY	70
2 A Sense of GRATITUDE	72
3 A Sense of MEMORY	74
4 A Sense of FORGIVENESS	76
5 A Sense of SERVICE	78
Welcome to the Way!	79

The Invitation

*They said to him,
"Teacher, where do you stay?"
Jesus answered, "Come, and see!"*
JOHN 1:38–39

You are starting out on a pretty important adventure. You are invited by the members of your parish to prepare for your confirmation in the Catholic faith. This invitation comes at a turning point in your life—a time when lots of things are changing. You are not a little kid anymore, but you're not too grown up either.

You are being asked to spend time preparing for Confirmation. What for? Well, this faith community—this parish—wants you to discover and enjoy the life everybody shares here—the life of the Spirit. They want you, with your youth and enthusiasm, to join them on the way of Jesus.

On the night before he died, Jesus told his friends that he was going on ahead of them. He told them that they already knew the way that leads to where he was going. Silence! The friends of Jesus were puzzled by what Jesus had just said. Thomas (that's right, *doubting* Thomas) piped up. "We don't know where you are going. How can we know the way?"

Even though this was one of those very solemn moments, Jesus probably broke out in one great big "Gotcha!" kind of smile. He probably looked right at Thomas and said, "*I* am the way, the truth, and the life."

WE WANT YOU WITH US

The people of this parish care that you meet Jesus and learn about his way. They care *about you*, respect you, and very much want you with them. The members of this parish want you to be an active and involved participant in everything they are about—in what they do, believe, and feel. So, they are welcoming you to the way—the way of Jesus Christ. And they are promising to understand you and support you.

Over the coming months, you will be doing a lot of thinking, sharing, praying, celebrating, caring, and growing. (And, according to plan, you will have a good time, too.) This preparation time is all about the way, about truth, and about life. Everybody in this parish wants you to be the best you can be. They feel that the way of Jesus Christ as it is lived out in this parish has a lot to offer you.

So, if you are willing, come on along. You will get some real support and understanding from the leaders of this process. You will have a special helper, or sponsor, to lean on. You will have the chance to say how you really think and feel. You will learn more about the way of Jesus. At the end of the process, you will receive a special gift—the Holy Spirit.

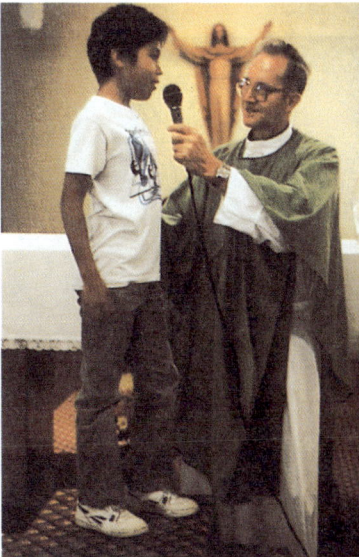

YOU ARE WELCOME

Welcome to the Way! has five parts to it:

1. *The Invitation:* The community welcomes you into the preparation process. (In case you haven't noticed, you are going through that part right now.)

2. *The Discovery:* This is a chance for you to look at what it means to belong to the Church.

3. *The Quest:* This is a chance for you to go and find out for yourself just how the Holy Spirit is working in your parish.

4. *The Rite:* This is a chance for you to see how the sacrament of Confirmation works.

5. *The Treasury:* This is a whole knapsack full of important things you might need along the way. So, welcome aboard! Welcome to the way!

The Discovery

*Let me assure you.
No one can see the reign of God
without being born again
of water and the Spirit.*
JOHN 3:5

Nicodemus was too scared to come to see Jesus during the daytime. Nicodemus was one of the leaders of the Jewish people, and he didn't want people to think that he was following this wandering teacher. He had a high position to protect. But Nicodemus was very curious. Something about this teacher made sense to him. He had to find out more.

So Nicodemus sneaked off to see Jesus in the dead of night. He left his home dressed in the simple clothes of a servant. He hurried to the garden where Jesus promised to meet him. He looked both ways before entering the garden. At the center of the garden was a well. As Nicodemus approached the well, he saw that Jesus was already there. Jesus jumped up to greet Nicodemus as an old friend greets somebody he hasn't seen for a long time.

The friendly greeting surprised Nicodemus, but the Jewish leader was still pretty nervous. He wasn't sure how to start. Jesus smiled and waited. Finally, Nicodemus blurted out, "Rabbi, er, ah . . . we know you are a teacher who comes from God because nobody could do the good things you do unless sent by God."

Jesus felt sorry for Nicodemus, so he stepped in. He began to tell Nicodemus about the wonders of God's love. He told him that everybody has the chance to be born in the Spirit—to become new—to belong to a new family. All through the night they talked. Nicodemus asked questions. Jesus answered them. How exciting this was! What discoveries Nicodemus was making! When the first light of dawn peeked over the mountains, Nicodemus had his biggest discovery burning in his heart. "God loved the world so much that God gave God's only Son, that whoever believes in him may not die but may have life—forever!"

You don't have to sneak off to a garden to talk with Jesus. This time of preparation for Confirmation is a chance for you to make some very special discoveries.

☐ You will discover *Jesus Christ*. Who is he? What does he mean for you?

☐ You will discover the *Holy Spirit*. This great power, friend, and gift is the very life of the Church.

☐ You will discover your *mission*. You are called for something special.

☐ You will discover the *Church*. You have a community that believes in you and supports you.

☐ And you will discover *ministry*. To belong to the Church means serving people and letting them serve you, too.

In each Discovery chapter, you will take four special steps.

1. You will discover things about *yourself*.

2. You will discover things about the *Good News*—the Gospel.

3. You will discover a lot about the *community*.

4. You will also be making some strong *connections* between what the faith is and who you are.

You will be given the chance to celebrate this faith, too. And you will keep a little Discovery Journal. So dig in and enjoy your discovery.

A PROMISE

In the space below, write a promise to throw yourself into the discovery process. Include some *reasons* in your promise. Don't be afraid to share your promise.

SELF

I
CHRIST

Close to Home

THE THOUGHTFUL PEASANT LIVED in a small village with his family. Day after day, he worked in the fields and cared for his family. Day after day, he noticed how oxen were beaten, families squabbled, field hands were overworked. The long summer evenings found his neighbors growing tired of the thoughtful peasant's passionate speeches against all these injustices.

By night, the thoughtful peasant dreamed of a world where love ruled, where work was creative, where food and drink and goodwill were plentiful.

One day, the peasant did not go to the fields. Instead, he packed a bedroll, put a meager supply of food in a sack, and told his wife he was going to search for the heavenly city. (You see, he was convinced there was such a place.)

Off he trudged. Day after day, he traveled—his eyes wide with anticipation. Every night, he made camp. And just so he would not lose

his way, he pointed his clogs in the direction he was headed. Then he would sleep—his dreams full to the brim with the wonders of the heavenly city.

One night, the thoughtful peasant was camping with a few scruffy travelers. A trickster among them waited until the peasant was asleep. Then he turned the poor man's clogs around and faced them in the opposite direction.

The peasant woke at sunrise, rolled up his bed, slipped into his clogs, and off he went down the road searching out the heavenly city that lay ahead. And not too many sunsets later, the peasant arrived at a small village washed by the dying sun. A pleasant village it was (although it was somewhat familiar).

The peasant knocked at the door of a whitewashed cottage. He was welcomed by a woman who looked just like the wife he left! It *was* the wife he left. How could this be? But there she was with his own small children. With hugs and kisses the crazy peasant was welcomed back. He settled again into the small cottage and lived in this heavenly place ever after.

DISCOVERING SELF

1. What do you like best about your life right now? What are two things you would like to change? Tell why.

2. What is *your* idea of a heavenly city? What would make your life *the best?*

News of a Messiah

THE JEWISH PEOPLE BELIEVED that God would not leave them alone. They believed that somehow, someday, in some way, a savior would come and set up a heavenly city in the middle of their homeland. But when the news of the Messiah came blowing in, there were very different reactions.

The Leaders. The leaders sometimes treated the news of the Messiah as bad news instead of good news. They thought they had everything under control. They knew God's Law—or thought they did. And they made sure that everybody obeyed. What did they need a savior for?

The Zealots. The Zealots were a political party that wanted to make lots of changes. They welcomed the news of a Messiah. But they wanted a Messiah who would lead them into battle. They wanted a political savior.

The Poor. When the poor people heard about a Messiah, they didn't know what to think. They had been disappointed so often. Most of all, these people were hungry and hurting. They wanted a savior who could give them food.

Everybody was looking for a Messiah who would make things right. Only nobody agreed what *right* was.

The Christ

The Good News of a Messiah took flesh in Jesus. Jesus wandered around Israel teaching and healing and forgiving.

He told the leaders of the people that they had to follow the Law, but they had to be merciful, too. He told them they had to become like little children.

Jesus told the Zealots that peacemakers were the really happy people. He told them that God is loving. He told them to melt down their swords to make plows.

Jesus told the poor that they could be happy, too. But not just because somebody gives them bread. He told them to look at the birds of the air and the flowers in the field. God really *cares* for people. God wants them to dance and to be happy and free.

Jesus told people, "I come as a gate open wide to the truth. I am a good shepherd who will guide my sheep. I am bread to feed empty hearts."

This was really Good News!

Jesus meant what he said. He was the Messiah—the Christ. He worked to change people's hearts. He comforted and healed. He changed the whole world and called it into God's blessing.

And he has never stoppped. He continues to do it now and forever.

DISCOVERING GOOD NEWS

1. What is your own personal picture of Jesus Christ? Share what you think he stands for (not what he looked like).

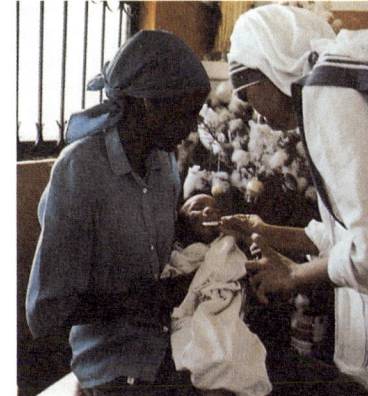

2. Now crack open a Bible, and read one of the passages listed below. What does this passage tell you about Jesus Christ?
- ☐ Matthew 5:1-15—a special sermon
- ☐ Mark 2:1-12—more than one kind of healing
- ☐ Luke 4:14-22—a message in the synagogue
- ☐ John 1:1-14—a powerful poem

Becoming Church

THE CHURCH IS A COMMUNITY of people who believe in and try to follow Jesus. You are part of that Church, and you have been invited to take that belonging very, very seriously. There will always be a place for you. You *will* fit in. Look around some Sunday. What do you see? The Church is chock full of wonderful people like these:

1. Inspector Ralph Martinson is forty-two years old. He has spent twenty of those years as an undercover officer in the vice squad of the Chicago Police Department. He has seen the seamy side of life.

2. Lizzie Pearl is a widow in her late sixties. Her garden is her pride and joy. Almost every evening you can see Mrs. Pearl rocking on her back porch as she oversees her green and growing domain.

3. Ben Fisher's hair is five inches long, red at the roots, black at the ends, and sticks straight out from his head. Part of the right side of his head is shaved. Ben also seems to have a guitar growing out of his hip—a guitar which produces some very heavy-metal sounds.

4. Melissa Rice graduated at the top of her class. The Cromwell Corporation hired her straight out of college to do computer chip design. Melissa is a career woman on the move.

How Are They Church?

These are pretty ordinary people. How are they following Jesus—besides just going to church? Take a look at what they do after church.

1. Inspector Martinson helped start a drug center. His efforts have helped scores of teenagers get off drugs—or never get started. The inspector says that while his work taught him that some people are dangerous, it also taught him that most people just need a break.

2. On the two nights a week Lizzie Pearl is not working in her garden or rocking on her porch, she is cooking up a storm at Saint Stephen's shelter for the homeless. "If I didn't have Saint Stephen's," she says with a grin, "I'd have to can or freeze all these veggies. And canning is a pain in the neck!"

3. Most Friday nights, you can find Ben Fisher hanging out at Butler Park Youth Center. A lot of other kids are hanging out there with him. All those kids are eleven years old. Ben is a Scout leader. He has taught several of his Scouts to play guitar, and they have even formed what Ben calls a "light-metal" band—Ben's Den.

4. The Cromwell Corporation wanted Melissa Rice to work on ways to build nuclear bombs. So, she quit and tries to work on her own. Between jobs, she tutors kids who have a tough time with math. And she does it for free.

The Church you are invited to is people like Inspector Martinson, Mrs. Pearl, Ben Fisher, and Melissa Rice. The Church is wherever strange and wonderful people like them come together in Jesus Christ. You are on the way with them.

DISCOVERING COMMUNITY

1. How do the people you see in church on Sunday make you feel like part of the community? (Be very honest!)

2. Where is the Messiah in your community? Who is peacemaking? Who is forgiving? Who is feeding the hungry? Who is helping the poor?

CONNECTIONS

Changing Things

DO A LITTLE EXERCISE. The star in the box below is you. Now think of four or five relationships that really matter to you. Write the initials of these people nearer to or farther from the star to show their importance in your life.

Then, look at the diagram you have created. Think about the relationships you would like to change in some way. Circle those initials.

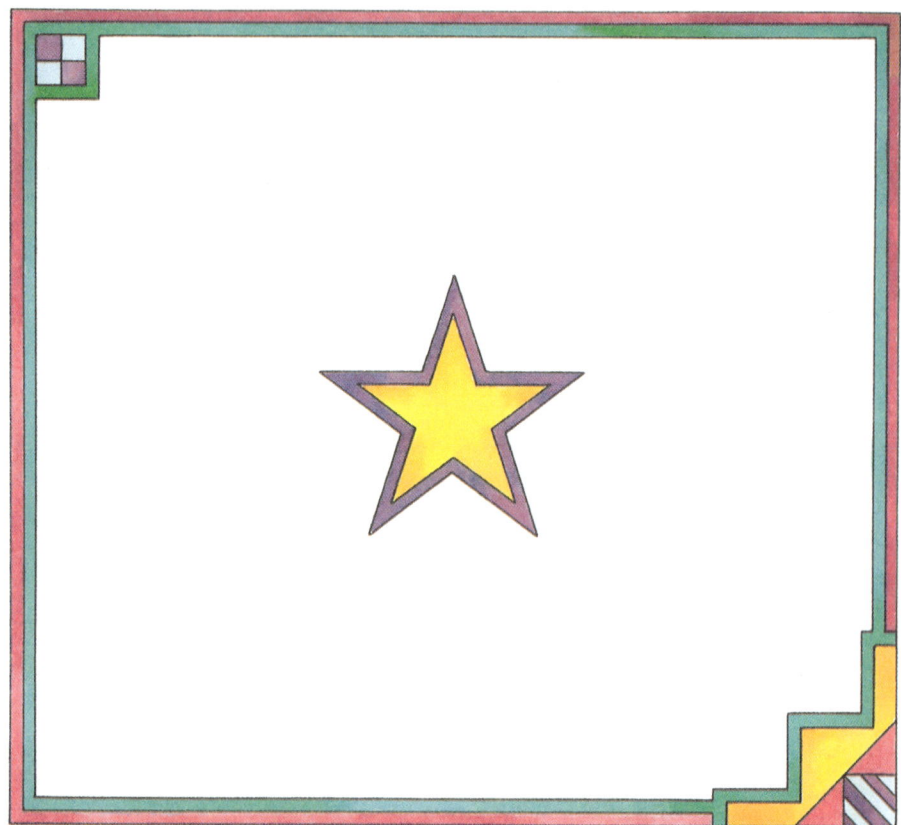

Now think about Jesus Christ. Would you put the initials JC on your diagram? Would you circle those initials? Be prepared to talk about your answer.

Finally, write two ways you can show that you are a follower of Jesus, the Messiah, and that you are a member of the faith community.

☐ _____
_____

☐ _____
_____

Celebrating Christ

JESUS HAS COME TO HELP you discover how to love yourself, others, and God by walking *together* on the way of faith. So, remember you are not alone. You are part of a strange but wonderful people who together are on the way, who have heard the Good News of Jesus.

The Prayer of Saint Francis

Lord, make me an instrument of your peace.
Where there is hatred, let me sow love;
   where there is injury, pardon;
   where there is doubt, faith;
   where there is despair, hope;
   where there is darkness, light;
   and where there is sadness, joy.

O Divine Master, grant that I may not so much
   seek to be consoled as to console;
   to be understood as to understand;
   to be loved as to love.

For it is in giving that we receive;
   it is in pardoning that we are pardoned;
   and it is in dying that we are born to eternal life.

DISCOVERY JOURNAL

Use this space to keep track of some of the discoveries you have made about Jesus Christ.

SELF

2
SPIRIT

People of Spirit

SOME PEOPLE SEEM TO BRIGHTEN up a party just by showing up. They walk into a room, and the room takes on a new life. Colors become brighter, and conversation gets better. These people of spirit cause things to happen. They give off sparks. They make things jump. People like to be around people of spirit. When they lead, they electrify crowds. Some of these people of spirit can jump-start whole groups. Everybody looks to this kind of leader for promise, optimism, and excitement.

Other people of spirit spread a calm and peaceful influence. They move slow and easy. They seem as durable as stone. People look to these spirited people for support and for strength. These strong, silent, and reflective people give steady guidance and understanding.

Some people of spirit bring out the best in those they meet. These spirited people give others a sense of goodness and worth. People matter to these spirited people. And so, they can inspire people to success. These people of spirit offer support and encouragement.

People who have these qualities of spirit have something in common. They *give* their spirit to others. And people feel goodwill, self-worth, challenge, and pleasure.

You know people of spirit. So, spend a minute doing a little mental exercise. Review the list of spirit qualities below. Then, for each quality, come up with one person you know who has this quality. You can dream up some spirit qualities on your own, too. Here's the list:

- ☐ Quiet
- ☐ Supportive
- ☐ Peaceful
- ☐ Generous
- ☐ Forgiving
- ☐ Lively
- ☐ Strong
- ☐ Daring
- ☐ Enthusiastic

DISCOVERING SELF

1. Imagine that someone has asked you to plan a field trip. What qualities would you draw on in yourself to make the trip a success?

2. Suppose a friend were in real trouble and needed someone to listen. What qualities in you would you rely on most to help your friend?

GOOD NEWS

The Gift

IN THE VERY BEGINNING, there was only darkness. Yet, above the darkness, the Spirit of God waited. From the beginning, the Spirit settled on this person or on that one—on ordinary people—filling them with power. The stories of the Bible tell the adventures of the Spirit.

Abraham and Sarah. The old couple felt at home. The land was fertile, and life was good. But the Spirit of God had other plans for Abram and Sarai. The Spirit led them to a land far from home. They followed the Spirit, and they were given new names—Abraham and Sarah. They were blessed with descendants as countless as the stars in the sky.

Moses. The shepherd looked at the burning bush. It was not burning up. Moses was face-to-face with God. He tried to tell God that he was not the one for the job. But the Spirit of God changed Moses. He was picked to lead the children of Israel out of slavery.

David. Like Moses, David was a shepherd. He was a singer who was happy living near Bethlehem. But the Spirit of God had other plans for David, too. The Spirit led David to be king of God's people. Even when David sinned, the Spirit of God did not leave. David was forgiven, and from his family would come the Servant King of heaven and earth.

Mary. Mary was a very ordinary girl in the town of Nazareth. She did her chores and thought about her future. She thought about life with her

husband. But the Spirit had other plans for Mary. A visitor from heaven came to her and told her she was going to be God's own mother. She was shocked, but she said yes. Mary became the Mother of the Promised One—the Mother of all. And through her yes, the Spirit spilled out over the whole earth.

Jesus. In Jesus—God's only Son—the Spirit found new ways to bring life and love to a cold world. After just a few years of teaching, Jesus was facing death. He was eating with his close friends for the last time. Without a word, Jesus got up, took water and a bowl, and washed the feet of his friends.

After he had finished, all eyes were on him. "My friends," Jesus said, "I want you to know that the greatest among you must be like the least. I give you a *new* commandment: *Love one another.* I really want you to love one another."

DISCOVERING THE GOOD NEWS

1. Get to know more about some of the biblical heroes you have just read about. Pick two or three of the passages listed below. Write some key words that tell what you discovered in your reading.

- ☐ Genesis 12:1–9, 17:1–8, 22:15–18—more about Abraham and Sarah
- ☐ Exodus 3:1–11, 4:10–17, 20:1–17—more about Moses
- ☐ 2 Samuel 12—more about David
- ☐ Luke 1:26–38—more about Mary
- ☐ Luke 3:21–22, 4:14–21; Matthew 5:1–12; John 13:1–15—more about Jesus

2. How can you discover the Spirit of God in your life—in your family, in your neighborhood, in your parish?

COMMUNITY

Spirit Power

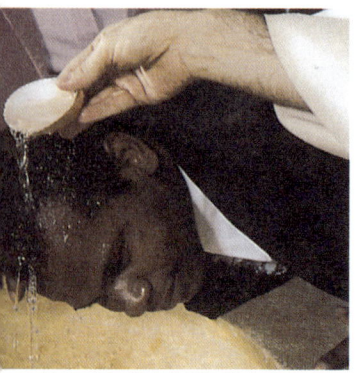

THE SPIRIT OF GOD does not come with movie magic or special effects. If you want to find the power of the Spirit, you need to look at people. You can start with the people in the Church to which you belong. The Church is made up of ordinary people—people who believe there is more to life than meets the eye. These people are convinced that the Spirit of God has plans for them.

You joined this group at your baptism. On that day, you tapped into the power of the Holy Spirit. And from that day on, the Church has tried to take care of you. It has done this by sharing with you the Word of God, its life as a community, and the meal Jesus left as a reminder.

The Word of God

The Church has kept alive the Word of God—the story of Jesus—and has shared that story with you. As you make that story more and more your own, it becomes part of your life. As you set goals and make decisions, you are now able to do so in light of the way Jesus lived and loved and acted. You can find the power of the Spirit in the Word of God.

The Community

The power of the Spirit is also found in the struggles of the Church to live as a community. A person does not have to be part of a church to care about others—to give first place to others. But it is one of the first rules of membership in the Church to care for others.

The power of the Spirit is discovered anytime the Church works to be an open community that welcomes and cares for all who come around. The power of the Spirit is there every time the Church stands with and reaches out to the deprived and the oppressed.

The Eucharist

The power of the Spirit is also evident in the way the Church regularly shares the meal Jesus shared. In the weekly Eucharist, the Church—the people on the way—gathers to celebrate the death and resurrection of Jesus. The Eucharist is a high point in the life of the Church community. What happens at the Eucharist is the work of the Holy Spirit.

- ☐ A people are united to one another and to God.
- ☐ The story of Jesus is shared and kept alive.
- ☐ A people share in the sacrifice of Jesus on Calvary.
- ☐ They are filled with strength and nourishment to live the new life Jesus gives.
- ☐ They reach out and serve others.

In all this, do not expect fireworks. Even here, the Spirit of God is gentle and quiet and wears a very human face.

DISCOVERING COMMUNITY

1. What is your biggest dream? How can the other members of the Church help you reach this dream?

2. Where do you see the power of the Spirit at work in your parish?

CONNECTIONS

Surprised by the Spirit

AS FOLLOWERS OF THE WAY, Christians are often surprised by the Spirit in their lives. But nobody will be surprised by the Spirit if they are not open to being surprised.

A simple two-step plan will help you become more aware of the Holy Spirit. The first step is *"Be still!"* Every day, set aside five minutes to be quiet, reflective, and open to the Spirit. Use the space below to make a simple pledge to pray every day.

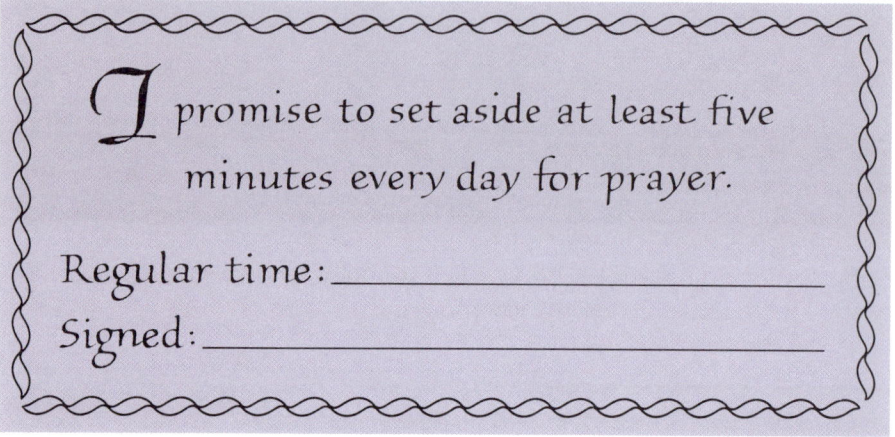

I promise to set aside at least five minutes every day for prayer.

Regular time: _____

Signed: _____

The second step is *"Be active!"* You can be sure that the Holy Spirit is with you whenever and wherever your actions are generous and directed toward others. In your activities, ask yourself the following questions:

1. Am I being true to the Good News?
2. Am I showing love?
3. Am I helping others?

If you can say yes to each question, you are acting in the power of the Spirit.

Use the space below to plan one action of the Spirit that you will do during the next week.

22

Celebrating the Spirit

THE POWER OF THE HOLY SPIRIT is yours to share. Use the following prayer often during the coming week.

Prayer of Trust

Gracious God,
You have looked into my heart.
You know me.
You know me when I sit or stand.
You understand my thoughts.
You know my plans.
You have great plans for me.
You know everything about me.
If I go up to the heavens, you are with me.
If I go down to the earth, you are with me.
If I soar on the wings of dawn or roam the seven seas,
　　still you are my guide.
You hold me close.
Lead me forever on your way.

BASED ON PSALM 139

DISCOVERY JOURNAL

Use this space to keep track of some of the discoveries you have made about the Holy Spirit.

SELF

3
MISSION

Angel's Journey

ANGEL FELT SAFE ONLY when he was on the move. His bike carrying him and the road flying by beneath him was all he needed. But Maria got to him—really got to him. She was the kind of friend who could make him stop running away.

But that was not so easy. He would have to stop being the big tough guy—the strong man nobody could hurt. And right now, Angel was hurting. He was afraid.

When he found the cassette on the seat of his motorcycle, Angel was confused. How did it get there? The soft, strong voice on the tape sent him out to the country—down the back roads. The voice guided him to a rickety old church.

The hissing from the back room drew him past the altar and down the hall. A television? A videocassette with his name on it? Who was playing a joke on him? It couldn't be Maria!

On the screen a story unfolded. The scene was so ordinary (almost too ordinary). There was this guy, Jeff, and this girl, Maggie. Jeff was a jock, and Maggie was a brain. ("What is going on here?" thought Angel.)

Anyhow, both were waiting for a ride. They were both interested in each other, but they had the wrong ideas. Jeff thought Maggie would be stuffy and brainy. She would—of course—put him down for being a dumb football player. Maggie was sure that a popular guy like Jeff would have nothing to do with her. Angel had to smile. This story could be about *him*. He just wasn't sure *how*.

Anyhow, Jeff finally got up the guts to talk to Maggie. She was okay. She was nice. She didn't like football or Gulliver's travels. She was warm and open. What a shock!

And she was really surprised about Jeff, too. He remembered her from math class. He didn't put her down. He didn't even laugh at her ignorance of football. Hey, wait! This is different—simple and scary.

Then Maggie's ride came. Jeff had to move fast. "What *do* you like?" he called out.

"Pizza," came the answer.

Then the screen went blank. The voice drew Angel's gaze closer. "Reality has a way of surprising us, doesn't it?" said the voice. "There's always more to the story if you're willing to look for it."

Angel had the feeling that he had not heard the last of this strange guardian.

DISCOVERING SELF

1. What do you fear the most? What would you risk the most for?

2. Angel, Jeff, and Maggie all had labels stuck on them. What are two or three labels that get in the way of the real you?

GOOD NEWS

Go for It!

THE FOLLOWERS OF JESUS were scared. The last three days had shaken them to the core. All their plans and dreams about Jesus seemed to be dead. So they sat huddled in a locked room, remembering—and hurting.

Thursday. The Passover supper was strange. The food was familiar. But what was Jesus doing with the bread? ("This is my body.") What was he doing with the cup? ("This is the cup of my blood.") And what did he mean when he said, "Do this in my memory"?

Later, in the cool garden, Jesus wanted to be alone. He wanted them to stay awake and pray. But they were too tired. The next few minutes were the worst! Judas came with soldiers. He kissed Jesus and said good-bye. Jesus was tied up and dragged away.

Everybody headed for the hills—except Peter and John. Jesus the storyteller was silent. Jesus who set people free was tied up. Jesus the friend was alone.

Friday. This was the preparation day for a holiday—a day to sweep and scrub. But the houses were empty. The air was hot with curses. "Crucify him! Crucify him!"

So they did. Jesus was hanging on a cross. His head tossed upward in search of a friend. The wind knifed across his body—the frozen blast of despair. "My God! My God! Why have you abandoned me?" Jesus, confident Son of the Father, was alone. "Father, into your hands I commend my spirit." Silence! Death!

Saturday. Of all the handpicked friends of Jesus, only John had firsthand memories. The rest did not see the sun break. They did not see the moon jump out of its path or the stars shatter into crystal slivers. They did not see the veil of the temple split and unravel. Hidden away, the followers of Jesus saw only that the world was ending for them. A sad and frightening Saturday passed.

Sunday. A new week began. The followers were so filled with their own fearful thoughts that they failed to notice the gentle stirring in the stuffy room. It was as if a springtime perfume had been sprinkled—a new, exciting, and waking smell.

Suddenly, Jesus broke the dark surface of terror and despair. "Peace!" he said. "As the Father has sent me, so I send you. Receive the Holy Spirit."

Filled with the Holy Spirit, the friends knew they had to go for it. They had to bring good news to all peoples—to lead them from doubt to faith, from fear to courage, from sin to reconciliation, from death to life. They had the strength of Jesus' last promise. "Know that I am with you always, until the end of the world."

DISCOVERING GOOD NEWS

1. Try to touch the feelings the Apostles had during those strange and wonderful last days of Jesus. Choose one of passages below. Write how you felt after your reading.
   - ☐ Matthew 26:17—28:20
   - ☐ Mark 14:12—16:20
   - ☐ Luke 22:1—24:53

2. How do you know that you share the mission of Jesus—what Jesus is all about? How do you know that Jesus believes in you—in what you are all about?

COMMUNITY

Peace Is with You

WHEN JESUS SAID "PEACE" to his friends, he was also saying it to you. And he is saying a mouthful. When Jesus says "Peace," he is saying, "God knows who you are, knows your failings and your fears, and loves you right in the middle of all that mess!"

God is with you not to condemn you—to get you for not being perfect. God doesn't love you in spite of everything that is wrong with you. God loves you! Period!

It can be pretty hard to believe that anybody loves you without any strings attached. But that is what the mission of Jesus is all about. And that mission has two parts.

1. *Be your best!* God loves you just the way you are, but that doesn't mean there is no room for hopes and dreams. You have lots of growing and changing to do. You have your own dying and rising to do. The nice thing is that you don't have to fill that tall order all alone.

2. *Share love and forgiveness!* The mission of Jesus means that you sink your teeth into life—your own and others'—and bring out the best in it. People who follow Jesus are open to loving others. It is as simple and as tough as that.

Down through the centuries, spirited people like you have accepted the mission of Jesus. In fact, the mission has created the people called Church. You are part of this mission-minded people. The whole people is bound together in the power and strength that comes from the Spirit of God.

DISCOVERING COMMUNITY

1. What is one thing you'd like to change in your life? How will you go about making this change? Who will help you make the change?

2. How does your parish live the mission of Jesus? How can you help? How can your parish help you?

CONNECTIONS

Catching Fire

DECIDING TO DO SOMETHING new is exciting—and scary. The first step is the worst step, yet the first step is also the best step. When people take that first step, they often catch fire, and the rest of the journey is a lot easier. When you decide to follow the way of Jesus, you take a first step. You commit yourself to a mission of being your best and of sharing love.

Let the circle below stand for an important decision—a first step—you can make as a Christian who has taken on the mission of Jesus. Write your single, important decision in the circle. On each ray marked with a plus sign, write one positive result of your decision. On each ray marked with a minus sign, write one negative result of the decision. Share the results.

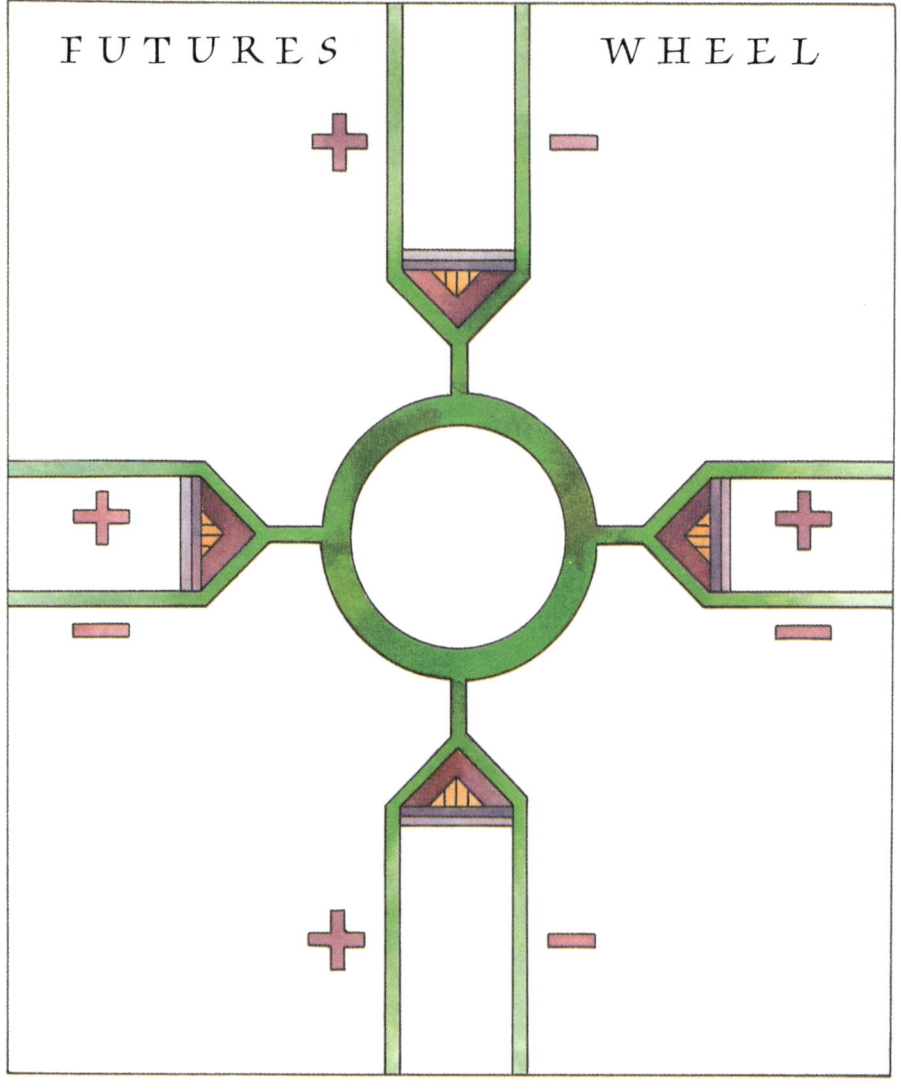

FUTURES WHEEL

Celebrating Mission

JESUS GAVE EVERYBODY who would follow him a very special mission prayer. Nobody can say this prayer *too* often.

> Our Father, who art in heaven,
>   hallowed be thy name.
> Thy kingdom come;
> Thy will be done on earth
>   as it is in heaven.
> Give us this day our daily bread;
> and forgive us our trespasses
>   as we forgive those
>   who trespass against us;
> and lead us not into temptation,
> but deliver us from evil.
> For the kingdom, the power, and the glory
>   are yours, now and forever.
> Amen!

DISCOVERY JOURNAL

Use this space to keep track of some of the discoveries you have made about the mission of Jesus Christ.

4
CHURCH

Testing the Waters

ANGEL ROARED INTO THE park. He knew Maria was there. Maybe he would have the courage to talk to her. But first he would listen to the words on the tape one more time. "That's right! I know about you," said the guardian voice. "Like the fact that people have let you down in the past. The truth is, you've confused being independent with being invulnerable."

From deep in the bushes came the hissing white sound of an untuned television—again. This time Angel was not so surprised.

The tape returned to the story of Jeff and Maggie. Jeff had decided to take Maggie out—sort of. He did not want to be seen with her. So he took her to a strange pizza parlor *way* across town.

They were alone in the place. The waiter was listening to old scratchy recordings of opera—loud, very loud. "A *big* pizza!" teased the waiter as he took their order. "That should thrill the palate."

Jeff and Maggie tried to get to know each other. But both of them were haunted by their fantasies.

Jeff saw his friend Troy—tending bar, of all things. "What's going on here?" said Troy. "Are you losing it? This girl is not your type. What are you hanging around her for? She is not going to give you what you are looking for."

"This guy is not even interested in you," said Maggie's friend Jennifer—from the blue. "Look at him! Is this the guy you want to spend your life with?"

Things were not going well at all. This was worse than that afternoon at school.

Jeff saw his mother at another table. (This was getting stranger and stranger.) "Take the risk, Jeff," she said. "Playing it safe is a lousy way to live—a lousy way to love."

Maggie excused herself and went to the rest room. In the mirror, she saw the image of her dad. "He seems like a nice kid, sweetheart," said the image. "Don't blame him for my mistakes—and I made some big ones." Then the image was gone.

Maggie returned to the table in tears. Jeff thought he had come on too strong. What was this all about? Getting to know somebody had to be easier than this.

Angel climbed back on his bike. Again he roared through the park. Maria caught sight of him. Would he ever come around? Would the guardian finish the story?

DISCOVERING SELF

1. Write whom you would turn to when you find yourself in each of the situations below.

   ☐ I want to have a good time.
   ☐ I want support for a decision I've made.
   ☐ I mess up and need to get back on track.

2. What qualities do you most value when you are looking to your friends for help? Their acceptance of you? Their common sense? Explain.

GOOD NEWS

A Day of Wind and Fire

IT WAS THE DAY OF the Jewish feast Pentecost, a festival which celebrated the first fruits of the spring harvest. Jerusalem was crowded with tourists. The Apostles and other followers of Jesus were once again gathered all together in a locked and shuttered room.

Suddenly, there came a rushing sound—like a strong, driving wind—followed by what appeared to be tongues of fire, which split and came to rest on the followers.

The Holy Spirit was dancing and calling the followers to join in the dance. Everyone present was filled with the power of the Spirit. The good news of the resurrection of Jesus came bubbling up out of them—news they just had to share.

Sharing Good News

Out they went into the crowded streets of Jerusalem. Fired by the Spirit, they began to tell anybody who would listen the good news. The city was crammed with foreign-speaking Jews. Amazingly, everybody understood the message the Apostles were shouting.

"These folks have been nipping at the new wine," some joked. "They're not saying anything. We're hearing only the babble of mid-morning drunks."

It just so happened that Peter heard this last remark. He stood up and called out, "My Jewish friends! Listen to me. We are not drunk with new wine of grapes. But, in a way, we are drunk with the good news of Jesus Christ."

Peter climbed on a ledge where everybody could see him. "What's the matter with you? Don't you recognize what the Prophet Joel told us?

'Pay attention. It is the Lord God who speaks to you: I will pour out my spirit on all humankind. Your sons and daughters shall prophesy. Your young shall see visions, and your old will dream dreams. Yes, I will pour out my spirit on everyone, and great signs shall appear in the heavens and on the earth. Then everyone who calls on the name of the Lord will be saved.'

"Look around you!" Peter cried out. "What Joel talked about is happening now! Change your lives and be baptized so that you may receive the Holy Spirit, too."

That very day, over three thousand people welcomed the Good News into their hearts, were baptized, and received the Holy Spirit. The mission was being handed on. The infant Church was starting to grow.

DISCOVERING GOOD NEWS

1. Read one or two of the passages listed below. They are from the Acts of the Apostles—the story of the ups and downs of the early Church. These passages tell of the best of times. Write your reactions.

- ☐ Acts 2:42–47—life in common
- ☐ Acts 4:32–35—caring for each member
- ☐ Acts 5:12–16—signs and wonders

2. Now read one or two of the passages listed below. They tell about the worst of times. Again, write your reactions.

- ☐ Acts 7:59—8:3—problems with outsiders
- ☐ 1 Corinthians 11:17–21—problems with insiders
- ☐ James 2:1–2—playing up to the rich and forgetting the poor

COMMUNITY

Not by Yourself

THE CHURCH IS A GROUP of people who have been called together to love. And the Church is the way for people to find God. The sharing that happens in the Church brings out the best in its members. It helps the members do what they do best—love one another, believe in the teachings of Jesus, and reach out to make the world a better place to live.

Filled with the Spirit, the early Church took shape. As you discovered in the Acts of the Apostles, the early Church shared the Word of God— the story of Jesus. They lived together as a loving community. They celebrated the meal Jesus left them. From the very beginning, the Church has tried to nourish its members by sharing its very best.

☐ *Baptism.* Your first share in the Church's best came at your baptism. Then you entered the experience of Christ's death and resurrection by having the water poured over your head. In Baptism, you also received the Holy Spirit.

☐ *Eucharist.* Every Sunday, you celebrate a meal of friendship and community—the Eucharist. The nourishment that the Church offers you is the Body and Blood of Jesus. The Eucharist gives you the strength to share the mission.

☐ *Confirmation.* In this sacrament, you share the experience of that day of wind and fire—Pentecost. You are empowered to reach out in service to others.

In the Parish

The Church is a huge, worldwide organization, but your experience of this community is right in your neighborhood. It is two subway stops, or four and a half blocks, or maybe seven cornfields away. It is the parish where people you know by name come to share and worship and grow.

The people of your parish join with millions of others around the world in welcoming the power of the Spirit, so that all together you can do ordinary things that just might have an extraordinary impact on your world. Together you can fill your world with joy and peace, lead a good and loving life, and even *live forever.*

DISCOVERING COMMUNITY

1. Why do you think it is better for you to belong to a parish than not to belong to one? (Be honest!)

2. Why is your parish a better place because *you* belong to it?

3. Explain one thing that makes it tough for you to be a member of the parish community.

CONNECTIONS

Take a Stand—Together

YOU READ ABOUT THE EARLY Church. You saw what the Holy Spirit was trying to do with those people. Well, that is what your pastor, the other ministers, and the people in your parish are trying to do, too. But nothing is perfect. Your parish is full of very ordinary and flawed people. That's the beauty of it. The declaration below is based on the Acts of the Apostles. Complete it! Share it! But most of all, *build* on it.

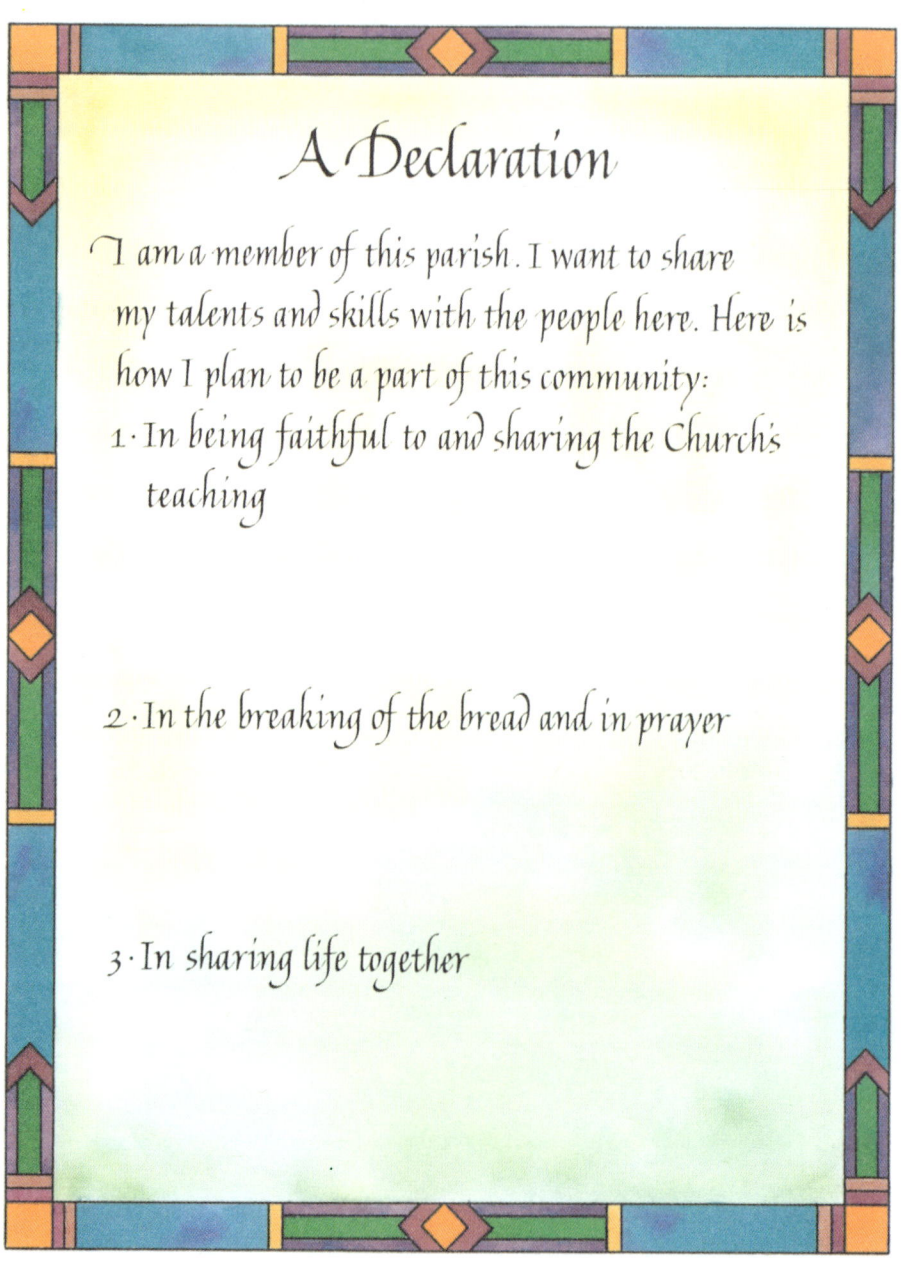

A Declaration

I am a member of this parish. I want to share my talents and skills with the people here. Here is how I plan to be a part of this community:

1. In being faithful to and sharing the Church's teaching

2. In the breaking of the bread and in prayer

3. In sharing life together

Celebrating Church

YOUR FAITH AND YOUR CHURCH are the same as those of the Apostles, the first believers and receivers of the Holy Spirit. Make the faith of the Apostles your own by praying the following this week.

The Apostles' Creed

I believe in God, the Father almighty,
Creator of heaven and earth;
and in Jesus Christ, his only Son, our Lord,
who was conceived by the Holy Spirit,
born of the Virgin Mary,
suffered under Pontius Pilate,
was crucified, died, and was buried.
He descended into hell.
On the third day he rose again.
He ascended into heaven,
sits at the right hand of God, the Father almighty;
from thence he shall come to judge
the living and the dead.
I believe in the Holy Spirit,
the Holy Catholic Church,
the communion of saints, the forgiveness of sins,
the resurrection of the body, and life everlasting.
Amen.

DISCOVERY JOURNAL

Use this space to keep track of some of the discoveries you have made about the Church.

5

Just Be You!

ANGEL PROPPED HIMSELF UP against the wall. He was more alone now than before. He did not like being invaded, bothered, pushed. He had to move. Down the street he walked without much direction—all the way to the open doorway, up the stairs. It was happening again. The room at the top of the stairs was as empty and unfurnished as Angel felt. The hissing sound drew him past the kitchen table and through the door. One more time Angel shoved the cassette into the machine.

Jeff found Maggie by her locker. He hadn't seen her for days. She was not very warm. "I've been sick . . . trouble with the phone . . .," she said.

"I am sorry about last week," Jeff began. I didn't mean . . ." Maggie moved away. Why was he trying so hard?

Jeff headed out to catch a ride. Then he waved the car away and burst back through the school door. "Maggie, I really want to talk. It is hard for me to talk to people I don't know. But I am not like that really."

Maggie looked at Jeff. "You really think this is your fault? It's not! It's me! I get so scared—scared I will say the wrong thing, scared I won't look right."

"But, Maggie," Jeff said, "you're not like the other girls. You laugh when something's funny. You're not afraid to not like football. You're not afraid to cry."

Jeff thought for a moment. "Let's pick a night—any night. On that night, you'll be you and I'll be me. And we won't worry about who sees us or what people think. We'll just be friends."

"That is the nicest invitation I ever got." A smile broke out on Maggie's face.

"Would you like to come to the dance with me on Saturday? Are you free?" Jeff asked.

"I promised to do something with Jennifer—I'll have to check," Maggie said.

"Invite her along!"

"Jennifer? The three of us? What will people think?" Maggie caught herself.

The wave of Jeff's hand told Maggie that this was going to be all right. They were going to be friends.

Could it possibly work? Angel hoped it was not too late. One more time he roared to the park. Maria was still there. The look on her face told Angel that this, too, was going to be all right. They were going to be *real* friends.

DISCOVERING SELF

1. Describe one time when pretending to be something you are not got you in trouble. How did it feel? What did you do?

2. Now describe a time when being yourself made it possible for you to help somebody. How did you feel then?

Gifted for Ministry

A THIN TRICKLE OF LIGHT wormed its way through the tiny barred window, splashing its rainbow glimmer into a corner of the prison cell. There sat a balding old man. He was scribbling furiously on every available inch of a ragged scroll. As the light traveled slowly across the room, the scribbler moved with it—a moth drawn to its flame. This was Paul—once Saul—of Tarsus. He knew the importance of light.

It had been so long since the light of Christ had knocked Paul off his horse on that dusty road to Damascus. With the light came a burning mission and a need to minister to others. Paul knew what he had to do. For more than fifteen years, Paul had crisscrossed the Mediterranean world, preaching and spreading the light to any and all who would receive it, treasure it, keep it ablaze.

Paul had used every scrap and talent and skill to spread the light. His knowledge of the Law and the prophets gave him a sure foundation. His own fiery drive and fervor made his task almost second nature. But Paul had gradually discovered other gifts that he did not know he had.

A newfound wisdom let him live in a more fully human way. His understanding seemed to increase, helping him to see the many ways God was working in him. He learned to make sound judgments, uncovering the *meaning* of people and events. As Paul's ministry grew, so did his knowledge. And his courage increased, too. He stood firm for his

beliefs, and he endured suffering because of them. Paul discovered a new reverence which cooled his hot temper and helped him look for the more prudent way to act. Paul also found himself in wonder and awe—daily more aware of God's bright presence—even in the dark of the dungeon in which he now sat.

Paul was sure that Christ's love would see him through. His pen flashed across the page.

> Who will separate us from the love of Christ? Can hard times separate us? Can pain or hunger or danger or nakedness or the sword separate us? No! I am absolutely certain that nothing can make Christ stop loving us. Nothing can separate us from Christ's care. Death can't do it. Powers of this world can't do it. Angels can't do it. Devils can't do it. Neither the present nor the future can do it. *Nothing.* Absolutely nothing in heaven or on earth can separate us from the love of God that comes to us in Christ Jesus, our Lord.
>
> ADAPTED FROM ROMANS 8:35–39

DISCOVERING GOOD NEWS

1. Read two of the passages about Saint Paul's ministry listed below. Write down what you *feel* about each one.

   ☐ 1 Corinthians 2:1–16—The cross is a stumbling block.
   ☐ Acts 13:13–49—Paul tries to be a light to the nations.
   ☐ Galatians 2:1–21 *or* Acts 15:1–29—The Church is for *everybody*.

2. You have the opportunity to ask Saint Paul one question about the Church (as *you* experience it). What will you ask?

COMMUNITY

Here to Help

AS YOU WANDER INTO CHURCH on Sunday morning, you could get the wrong idea about ministry. You see the priest at the altar, you see readers, and servers, and Eucharistic ministers, and ushers, and choir members. You might figure that *ministry* is just about *doing* something in church. Not so!

Ministry is not just a church word—it is a *life* word. Bishops and priests and deacons have their special work to do. It is official, and it is important. But all members of the Church have work to do—just as official, just as important, and usually very different.

Take a look at some of the ways ministry happens in the very ordinary neighborhood around Saint Patrick's Church.

1. Bob and Karen Nelson both work. They have a young family—two kids in junior high and one in preschool. Once a week, eleven seventh graders invade the Nelson home. For about an hour, the Nelsons talk and listen to these young people. Bob and Karen are volunteer catechists for their parish. They feel it is important to *do* something to keep their faith alive.

2. Polly McDonnell is a widow whose children are all grown up. She has lots of friends and enjoys giving and going to parties. Every Sunday evening, Polly and Fred Curtiss go to the Valley Shelter. There they serve dinner to the homeless. These homeless people are their friends. So, they sit and chat with these people until curfew.

3. Grover Washington is a vice-president of production at the TelDek Corporation. He has to meet schedules, solve problems, and keep up with a sea of paperwork. With Sharon Keller, a fellow executive, he

started inviting a group of the managers to a weekly breakfast. At this breakfast, the group spends a few moments in prayer. Most of all, they talk about ways to make the workplace a just, safe, and humane place.

4. Junior high school can be a pretty hostile place. There are lots of chances to get into trouble. After one youth ministry meeting, Carmen Salazar and Jerry Sigman decided to start a special club at Thomas Mann Junior High. They call their club WSS. *WSS* stands for "We Stay Straight." The members help one another stay out of trouble. WSS now has forty-six members.

DISCOVERING COMMUNITY

1. Right now, how do you serve others? How do others serve you?

2. What is one problem in your school that you could do something about? What could you do?

3. Describe someone in the community who is really reaching out to others.

CONNECTIONS

We Need You

WHEN YOU ARE FACED with a real need, ask yourself two simple questions: "If not me, who? If not now, when?"

Join up with a partner. Then, talk about the need each of you listed in the previous section. Pick one of the two as a project to work on. In the space below, describe it, and then write a plan of action. Ask yourselves the following questions.

☐ Does this plan fit in with the Good News of Jesus?

☐ Does this plan show love?

☐ Will this plan help others?

☐ Who will help us get started?

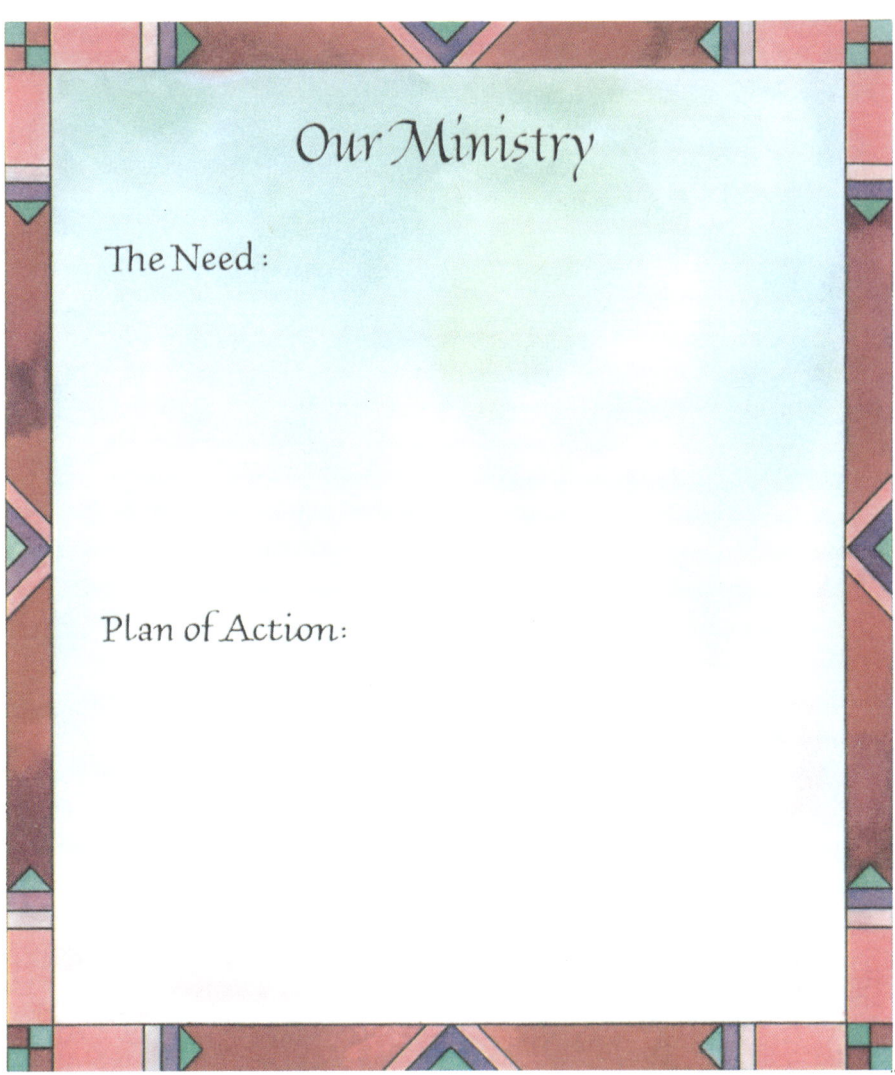

Our Ministry

The Need:

Plan of Action:

Celebrating Ministry

DURING THE CELEBRATION OF Confirmation, the bishop prays the words below. Take time every day this week to say this prayer yourself. It may help you discover your own gifts.

Prayer for the Spirit's Gifts

All-powerful God, Father of our Lord Jesus Christ,
>   by water and the Holy Spirit
You freed your sons and daughters from sin
>   and gave them new life.
Send your Holy Spirit upon them
>   to be their Helper and Guide.
Give them the spirit of wisdom and understanding,
>   the spirit of judgment and courage,
>   the spirit of knowledge and reverence.
Fill them with the spirit of wonder and awe
>   in your presence.
We ask this through Christ our Lord.
Amen.

DISCOVERY JOURNAL

Use this space to keep track of some of the discoveries you have made about serving others.

The Quest

John's disciples asked,
"Are you the one to come, or is there another?"
Jesus answered,
"Report to John what you hear and see."
FROM MATTHEW 11:3–4

The disciples of John the Baptizer had heard about Jesus. There were rumors everywhere about his power, his healing, his teaching. They were curious about Jesus. They had to find out for themselves. So, a group of them came to Jesus to find out if all the rumors were true. Maybe, just maybe, this Jesus was the promised Messiah.

Jesus did not waste too much time telling these visitors about himself. Instead, he told them to report on what they saw and heard. And what did they see and hear? They saw the blind recover their sight. They saw cripples walk. Lepers were cured. The deaf could hear again. The dead were raised to life. And (most important) the poor had the Gospel preached to them.

Their quest was a success. The disciples of John saw real evidence that God was with the people—that the promises were being fulfilled.

You are about to go on a quest, too. It is not enough for you to sit back and learn about your faith from the words of a catechist or from a book. Instead, it is time for you to be like the disciples of John—to go out and see for yourself.

On this quest, you will be looking for the way the Holy Spirit is at work in your community. This quest is the chance for you to dig under the surface of your parish. There you will find just how the gifts of wisdom, understanding, good judgment, courage, knowledge, reverence, wonder and awe—the same gifts Saint Paul had—are operating right under your nose.

Don't expect that these gifts are going to jump right out at you. And don't count on them being all dressed up in "holy" language. But at the end of the quest, you will see the same kind of evidence the disciples of John saw when they went on a quest to find the Messiah.

This is a rare opportunity. So, use the time wisely and well. The success of your quest is up to you.

PROMISE

In the space below, write a promise to take this quest seriously. Show your willingness to throw caution to the wind and really get into this process. Be willing to share your promise.

WISDOM

SURVEYING WISDOM

1. *Sound Quest.* Listen to the Sound Quest. Remember, "The Lord gives wisdom" *(Proverbs 2:6).*

2. *Definition.* Complete the following sentence: "She is as wise as . . ."

   _____

   _____

3. *Picture wisdom.* In the space below, draw a picture of what you think a wise person looks like.

SEARCHING FOR WISDOM

1. *Explore the Bible.* The Scriptures have a lot to say about wisdom. Some books of the Bible are called the Wisdom Books. Find and record some words of wisdom in each of the following books.

a. Psalms

_____

_____

b. Proverbs

_____

_____

c. Wisdom

_____

_____

2. *Decide for yourself.* Now write some words of wisdom that are all yours. Make them words you would like to live by.

_____

_____

3. *Find a wise person.* With the help of your sponsor, find a wise person. Meet with and interview that person. If possible, tape-record your interview. Share the results. If you want to, report about a public person who shows wisdom.

4. *Wisdom story.* You are beginning a Quest Scrapbook. Find a story in a newspaper or magazine that tells about wisdom or a wise person. Cut it out and tape it to this page so it won't get lost.

5. *Pray for wisdom.* Take time each day to say the following prayer for the Spirit's great gift of wisdom.

O God,
Grant me wisdom from the inside out.
Help me see beneath and within,
   betwixt and between.
Help me learn that there is
   more to life,
   more to others,
   more to you
   than meets the eye.
Amen.

2
UNDERSTANDING

SURVEYING UNDERSTANDING

1. *Sound Quest.* Listen to the Sound Quest. Try to really feel the words and the music. Ask, "Give me understanding so I may keep your Law with all my heart" *(Psalm 119:34).*

2. *Checklist.* Put a check by the qualities you would expect to find in a person who has the gift of understanding.

    ___ brains   ___ leadership   ___ drive

    ___ gentleness ___ strength   ___ forgiveness

3. *Tracking your language.* Keep track of how many times in one day you use the words "I understand" or "I don't understand." What did you mean when you used those words?

SEARCHING FOR UNDERSTANDING

1. *Listen up!* "Turn that darn thing down! How can you listen to that junk?!" Sound familiar? One of the hottest areas of misunderstanding between parents and teens is over musical tastes. Search for some understanding between your taste in music and your parents'. Choose one of your favorite recordings, and have your parents choose one of theirs. Agree to listen to one another's tune until you can at least hum it from memory. See what happens.

2. *Reach an understanding.* Every family has rules. What's one rule that causes hassles in your family—between you and your folks or other family members? Bedtime? Television? Chores? Privacy? Ask everyone involved if you can discuss the rule, change it, or come to some new understanding. Remember, this is an attempt to reach an understanding, not an excuse for battle. Keep track of what happens.

3. *Find an understanding person.* With the help of your sponsor, find a person who has the gift of understanding. Meet with and interview this person. If possible, tape-record your interview. Share the results. If you want to, you can report about some public person who shows the gift of understanding.

4. *Understanding story.* Here is another item for the Quest Scrapbook. Find a story in a newspaper or magazine that tells about understanding or about an understanding person. Cut it out and tape it to this page so it won't get lost.

5. *Pray for understanding.* Every morning, when you brush your teeth, take a good look at yourself in the mirror and pray:

Good God,
Help me to understand the truth about myself,
no matter how good it is.
Amen.

3
JUDGMENT

SURVEYING JUDGMENT

1. *Sound Quest.* Listen to the Sound Quest for the gift of judgment. This one is tricky, so pay attention to both the words and the music. "How wonderful is the Lord's judgment" *(Isaiah 28:29).*

2. *Decision list.* In the space below, list three decisions you have made in the past twenty-four hours. How did you go about making those decisions?

SEARCHING FOR JUDGMENT

1. *Help make a judgment.* A good friend shows up at your front door. The friend has obviously been drinking. You find out that the friend has stolen something from his or her parents' liquor cabinet. Your friend is not feeling so good and wants you to hide him or her until the effects of the drinking have worn off. What would you do? Why?

2. *Judgment in Scripture.* Read Matthew 25:31–46. Then answer the following questions.
    a. Do you think that the king in Jesus' story was too rough in his judgment? Why or why not?
    b. In what way do you think the people in the story—not the king—are the ones making judgments?
    c. How hard is it to do and to be your very best? Be specific.

3. *Find a person of judgment.* With the help of your sponsor, find a person in the parish who has good judgment. In what way does that person create and choose the good in difficult situations? How does he or she act as a person who is responsible? Meet with and interview the person. Tape-record the interview if you can. You may choose some public person to report on if you wish.

4. *Judgment story.* Here is another entry for your Quest Scrapbook. Find a story in a newspaper or magazine that tells about good judgment or about a person who has good judgment. Cut it out or copy it. Tape the copy to this page so that you don't lose it.

5. *Pray for judgment.* It is hardly ever easy to make good judgments. Even Jesus turned to God in prayer when he was faced with difficult decisions. Take time each day to pray for the gift of judgment.

Just and caring God,
teach me to tell the difference between
good and bad,
right and wrong.
But more than that,
show me the good way,
the right way—*your Way*—
in all the judgments I make.
Amen.

4
COURAGE

SURVEYING COURAGE

1. *Sound Quest.* Listen to the Sound Quest for the gift of courage. Remember that courage can be great or small. As you listen, "let your heart be bold and wait for the Lord" *(Psalm 27:14).*

2. *Courageous qualities.* Look at the word *courage* below. Cross each letter in the word with a word describing the qualities of courage.

```
              C
              O
        G  U  T  S
              R
              A
              G
              E
```

3. *It takes courage.* List three things in your life right now that you think take a lot of courage.

   a. _____

   b. _____

   c. _____

SEARCHING FOR COURAGE

1. *Courage in Scripture.* Jesus had courage, and so did Saint Paul, Abraham, Sarah, Moses, David, and Mary. The Bible is full of people—ordinary people—who had the gift of courage. Read all the passages below. Keep track of your reactions and be ready to discuss them.

    a. Judith 8:9–27—a beautiful widow's courage in the face of national despair

    b. Matthew 15:21–28—the courageous Canaanite woman

    c. Acts 7:55–60—Stephen, a man of special courage

2. *Find a courageous person.* With the help of your sponsor, find a person of real courage in the parish community. Remember that this courageous person does not need to be somebody who makes a big splash. He or she can have quiet and hopeful courage. Interview this person. Tape the interview or take notes. If you have trouble finding a private person of courage, write about some public figure.

3. *Courage story.* Find a story about courage or about a courageous person. Use newspapers, magazines, or television. Tape a copy of the story you find to this page, or write a brief report of the story in the margin of this page.

4. *Pray for courage.* Courage is not adrenalin. It isn't automatic or triggered by electrical impulses in the brain. Courage is an impulse of the heart. Pray each day for courage and a strong but open heart.

> Bold and courageous Lord,
> I mean to love, but don't dare to love.
> I dream big dreams, but seldom make them
>   come true.
> I plan to charge ahead, but only retreat.
> I pretend to be big and tough, but I am afraid of
>   little things—the opinion of others,
>   the laughter of friends, the disappointment
>   of parents.
> Encourage me, Lord.
> Strengthen me to give my whole heart to the
>   love, dreams, plans, and people I hold dear.
> Amen.

5
KNOWLEDGE

SURVEYING KNOWLEDGE

1. *Sound Quest.* Listen carefully to the Sound Quest for the gift of knowledge. Remember, knowledge has nothing to do with how *smart* you are. Instead, "the earth shall be filled with the knowledge of the Lord" *(Isaiah 11:9).*

2. *Picture, picture.* When Leonardo da Vinci painted the *Mona Lisa,* he did more than capture the outside of an Italian Renaissance woman. He opened a window to the woman's soul, and people have been trying to get to know her better ever since. On a small scale, see if you can do what da Vinci did. In the margin, draw a picture of you. Show by this picture how well you know yourself. Share the picture.

SEARCHING FOR KNOWLEDGE

1. *Get to know your family.* Set aside at least an hour when you can have your parents, brothers and sisters, guardians—the people who make up your family—all to yourself. Have everybody (including yourself) answer the three questions below. Then share the answers.
    a. What is one thing you know about each family member that he or she does not *think* you know?
    b. What is one thing you would like to know about each member of the family?
    c. What is one thing about *you* that you would like each member of the family to know?

2. *Get to know your faith.* The more you know about your faith, the better you can identify with the Catholic community. Find out at least *three*

things about the faith that you never knew before. They can be little things, or they can be very important. But they have to be *new*. On the lines below, summarize what you learn.

a. _____

b. _____

c. _____

3. *Get to know your parish.* Lots of people are involved in your parish. Lots of things go on. During this part of the quest, find out as much as you can about your parish—priests, deacons, lectors, cantors, servers, catechists, sisters. Get to know the organizations and committees, too—parish council, social justice committee, finance, maintenance, worship, education. Keep track of what you learn.

4. *Find a person of knowledge.* With the help of your sponsor, find somebody in the community who has the gift of knowledge. In what way does this person invite people into conversations? How does this person keep seeing people, ideas, and things in new and different lights? Interview this person of knowledge. Be sure to record somehow the results of the interview.

5. *Knowledge story.* Here is another item for the Quest Scrapbook. Find a story about the gift of knowledge—especially how it was used to *help* others. Tape a copy of the story to this page, or you can write a summary of the story in the margin.

6. *Pray for knowledge.* When you say "I want to know you," you are saying that you want to get closer to another. Prayer is a way to get closer to God. It is a way to *know* God.

Intimate God,
You know me inside out.
You know me as I am for who I am.
Help me grow to know others as you know me,
to know you as you know me.
Teach me to treasure the mystery of creation,
    your people, and yourself,
so that when I meet you face-to-face,
I may hear you say, "Hey, I *know* you!"
Amen.

6
REVERENCE

SURVEYING REVERENCE

1. *Sound Quest.* Let the words and music get you set for your search for reverence. Remember that reverence is not something from the head—"reverence the Lord Christ in your heart" *(1 Peter 3:15).*

2. *Poet's corner.* Are you a poet but don't know it? Now is the time to show it. On the lines below, try writing a form of poetry called *cinquain* about reverence. (This kind of poem has five lines.)

   a. Line one is the word *reverence.* (There, you have a head start.)
   b. Line two is two synonyms for reverence.
   c. Line three is three antonyms.
   d. Line four is a four-word sentence describing reverence.
   e. Line five is the name of someone you think is reverent.

   _____

   _____ _____

   _____ _____ _____

   _____ _____ _____ _____

   _____

SEARCHING FOR REVERENCE

1. *The spice of life.* Read Matthew 2:1-11—the story of three men who went a long way to show their reverence. As a sign of their reverence, these men brought fragrant spices. As part of your quest, find a spice whose

smell speaks of reverence to you. Discover something about the spice (where it comes from, how it is used). Bring a sample to the next session, where it will be used in a reverent way.

2. *Rock and reverent roll.* "The trouble with kids today is their blatantly irreverent music!" Heard that one before? As you know, it's not always easy for the generations to understand one another's musical tastes, but it is not impossible. To tell the truth, lots of kids themselves disagree on what is *the* radical music. Part of your quest this time is to find a tune from *your* kind of music that portrays or encourages reverence. (It can be awesome and fresh and still be reverent.) Bring a recording of the tune with you to the next session.

3. *Find a reverent person.* With your sponsor's help, find somebody in the parish who has the gift of reverence. Interview this person. Be sure to keep track of what you find out. If you wish, you can report about some famous person who has the gift of reverence.

4. *Reverence story.* Time for the Quest Scrapbook again. Find a newspaper or magazine story that tells about reverence. Tape a copy of that story to this page. Remember, reverence is a gift that means more than just acting holy.

5. *Pray for reverence.* Take time—even a little time—to think of God, to love God, and to grow in reverence.

Oh Holy One,
my treasure, my heart's desire,
teach me respect and joy for the work of your
   hands.
Offer me a portion of your compassion.
Teach me to recognize that everything you
   fashion is good.
Amen.

7
WONDER AND AWE

SURVEYING WONDER AND AWE

1. *Sound Quest.* Listen to the words and the music. "Reverence the holy One and be in awe of the God of Israel" *(Isaiah 29:23).*

2. *No small thing.* Wonder and awe are experienced in many different ways. Look at the word pairs below. Circle the word in each part that speaks to *you* of wonder and awe. Then share your choices with a partner. (There are no right answers, by the way.)

turmoil/peace	plain/fancy	freedom/law
safe/risky	asking/thanking	outward/inward
visible/invisible	feeling/belief	uncommon/common
solemn/joyful	giving/taking	structure/chaos
alone/together	nature/big city	familiarity/adventure

SEARCHING FOR WONDER AND AWE

1. *Wonder and awe in Scripture.* Scripture has lots of examples of the Spirit's gift of wonder and awe. Read two of the passages listed below. How do they tell you about wonder and awe?

   a. Psalm 136—a litany of wonder
   b. Matthew 9:1-8—the wonder of healing and forgiveness
   c. Luke 5:1-11—catching fish and catching people
   d. John 6:30-41—an awesome promise
   e. Acts 3:1-10—a wonderful cure

2. *Expressing wonder and awe.* If God were to appear to you in a burning bush or knock you off your feet with a shot of light on your way to the hamburger joint, you might not have a lot of trouble responding. It's a good bet, however, that you haven't met a lot of burning bushes or been struck too often by divine lightning. The experience of the gift of wonder and awe is not the same for everybody. And it is not always easy to talk about. Even so, it is generally something that seeks to be shared. At the next meeting, come ready and willing to share a personal experience of wonder and awe. You may use anything you want to help you share—a poem of yours or of somebody else's, a piece of music, a dance, a prayer, a painting or sculpture, a story of yours or of somebody else's.

3. *Find a person of wonder and awe.* With your sponsor's help, find and interview someone who has the gift of wonder and awe. In what way does that person draw you and others into the adventure of living? Don't forget to record the interview in some way. You can write about a public figure if you want to.

4. *Wonder and awe story.* Time for one last clipping for the Quest Scrapbook! Find a story that tells of the gift of wonder and awe. Tape a copy of the story to this page. If the story you find can't be copied, write a summary of it somewhere on this page.

5. *Praying for wonder and awe.* The experience of the gift of wonder and awe most often moves people to respond with prayers of praise. Take time to do that, too.

God of wonders and wonderful promises,
electrify me with but a hint of your
    awesome power.
Excite me with the adventure that is you,
    especially as it unfolds in my adventures
    with others.
Brighten my life with an awareness of you,
    so that I might sparkle and glow with the
    luster of love.
Amen.

The Rite

*All were filled with the Holy Spirit.
They began to express themselves
and make bold statements
as the Spirit prompted them.*

ACTS 2:4

Pentecost—the day of wind and fire—saw the Holy Spirit given to the brand-new Church. The people in this group—Peter and the rest—had now experienced both the presence of the Risen Jesus and his Holy Spirit. These remarkable experiences fired them to begin at once to spread the Good News that Jesus was Lord.

As more and more people heard and accepted the message of these Spirit-charged followers, they expressed a desire to become part of their dynamic group. The Apostles realized that new members would have to experience what they had experienced—the death and resurrection of Christ and the sending of the Holy Spirit.

Because the Apostles had shared in the death and resurrection of Jesus, they also had shared in Jesus' passage to new life. Because they had experienced the outpouring of the Holy Spirit, they also shared the mission of Christ and Spirit-given power to take on that mission. The Apostles knew that they had to share these life-changing experiences with others in some concrete way. What the Apostles did was to look at the actions of Jesus himself to find ways of welcoming others into their community. What they found were baptism and the laying on of hands.

A LITTLE HISTORY

Through baptism, candidates entered sacramentally into the experience of Christ's death and resurrection. They also received the Holy Spirit, who set them on the way of Jesus. By the laying on of hands, the new members entered into the experience of Pentecost. They were empowered by the Holy Spirit to bring others to Christ by their dedicated care and service.

These experiences were not just for individuals, they were also the way to create the community—the Church.

Over the years, as the Church grew, the community realized that the sacrificial meal left by Jesus was another special action and experience in which new members should share. So it happened that right after baptism and the laying on of hands, the new members were also welcomed to share in the Lord's Supper. Sharing the Body and Blood of the Lord became the sign of full membership in the Spirit-filled Church.

In the early days, these three actions took place all at one time—usually at the Easter Vigil. This way is still used in the Rite of Christian Initiation of Adults. Over the years, the three actions got separated. But they are still very much the actions of joining the Church. In much of North America, the Church celebrates the sacrament of Confirmation in junior high school. That is why you are getting ready for the sacrament of Confirmation now, while some of your friends may have celebrated it when they were younger.

The sacrament of Confirmation you are about to receive links you directly with the experiences of the Apostles. You have already experienced baptism and First Communion. Now you will experience the laying on of hands. You are going to be confirmed in the Holy Spirit.

PROMISE

In the space below, write a promise to participate in the celebration of Confirmation. Promise to bring your heart and your mind (as well as your body) to the sacrament. Share your promise so that your fellow candidates can help you keep it.

CONFIRMED IN THE SPIRIT

Celebrating Confirmation

ORDINARILY, THE BISHOP PRESIDES at the celebration of Confirmation. The presence of the bishop reminds everybody of the link to the Apostles at Pentecost. Your encounter with the bishop joins you to the Church.

The sacrament of Confirmation is usually celebrated during the Eucharist. That is how the community shows that *both* Confirmation and Eucharist are part of a person's initiation.

Here is a simple map to take you through the celebration. If you understand this map, you will have a very good idea of how the celebration works.

1. The celebration begins with a gathering followed by a Liturgy of the Word. Through God's Word, both the power of the Spirit and the will of God will be revealed to you.

2. After the Gospel, the pastor, deacon, or catechist presents you and your fellow candidates for Confirmation to the bishop. Your name will be

 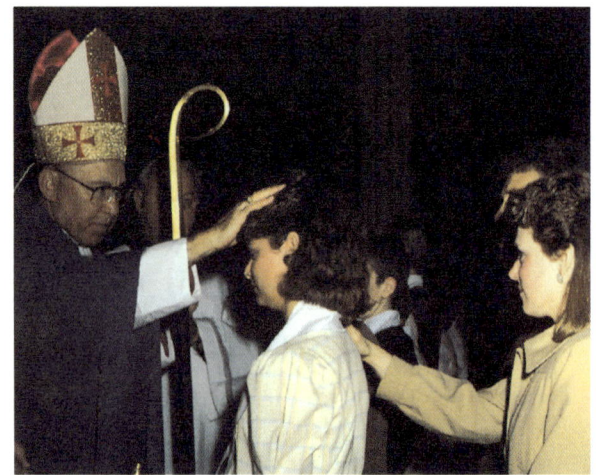

called. With your sponsor, you will stand before the bishop. For a few moments, the bishop speaks about the great gift of God's Holy Spirit and challenges you to take your place among God's People.

3. Since you have already become a member of the Church through Baptism, and to show the link between Baptism and Confirmation, the bishop will invite you to renew the promises made at Baptism. He will invite you to profess the faith you have in the Church.

4. The bishop invites the pastor and any other priests present to gather around him. Then he will say the following:

"My dear friends, in Baptism God our Father gave the new birth of eternal life to his chosen sons and daughters. Let us pray to our Father that he will pour out the Holy Spirit to strengthen his sons and daughters with his gifts and anoint them to be more like Christ, the Son of God."

5. The bishop and priests extend their hands over you in the great gesture of laying on of hands. Listen well as the bishop calls upon God to give the Spirit's sevenfold gifts. Those gifts have a lot of personal meaning for you now.

6. The bishop takes the chrism in hand. Chrism is the oil of priests, prophets, and kings. It is rich and smells wonderful. It is the same oil with which you were anointed at your baptism. The bishop calls you by name and anoints your head in the sign of the cross.

7. Together you all celebrate the Eucharist. You take your place with all the members of the Church around the Table of the Lord. You share in the Body and Blood of Jesus. You recommit yourself to the generous service of the Church and of the world.

With the rest of the fully initiated, you are setting out together on the way of Jesus.

BE THERE

What are two or three practical ways for you to make sure that you are really *there* during this celebration? How can you and your fellow candidates support one another?

The Treasury

*Store up heavenly treasure,
which neither moths nor rust corrode
nor thieves break in and steal.
Where your treasure is, your heart will be.*
MATTHEW 6:20–21

Maybe all this preparation is leaving you just a little limp in the head. "It seems so complicated! There seems to be so much to believe, to know, to care about as far as the Church is concerned. How can anybody be a good Christian and still have time to live—to get good grades, to play on the basketball team, to go to movies, to plan for the future? There are millions of things to do in life. Church is just part! Right?"

Wrong! The biggest mistake you could make would be to *separate* Church and life. You have been welcomed to the way of Jesus because the faith is a way to live. Getting good grades, playing basketball, and going to movies can all be part of your faith. Faith—like life—is not lived all at once. It unfurls a little at a time.

The pope and bishops have as their ministry to teach and preserve the Scriptures and the whole history of teachings. Everybody in the Church has the ministry of *living and believing* what the Church teaches. But again, you can't do that all at once.

You are going to make mistakes! That is for sure. But it really helps if you have some hooks to hang on to. It really helps if you look at some very basic realities about being a Catholic. That's what this Treasury is all about. It shows that learning and growing is lifelong, but there are some pretty basic notions about being a Catholic.

This Treasury shows you five very basic senses that the followers of Jesus share—from Pentecost to today. These senses will help you keep in touch with your feelings and with your Church. Learn them well, and promise to keep them alive in you!

PROMISE

In the space below, write a promise to master the material in this Treasury. Be willing to accept support in your resolution and to support the resolutions of others.

I

A SENSE OF
THE HOLY

Rachel's Blanket

THREE-YEAR-OLD RACHEL MANAGED to keep quiet during the last part of Mass—just barely. As Mass ended, Rachel made a quick backward sign of the cross and headed for the door.

She could not even be tempted by a Sunday morning doughnut. "I just got to get home!" she exclaimed.

As soon as the front door was opened, Rachel hightailed it into her bedroom. Suddenly, there was Rachel. "Lookit! Lookit!" she shouted.

"I see! I see!" Rachel's mother replied. "But what's all this excitement about your old blue blanket?"

Rachel twirled the blanket over her shoulders and poked her curly head through one of the blanket's many holes. "At church, Mommy," Rachel sparkled, "everybody sang about my blanket."

Rachel began to pirouette around the room, the tattered blanket flying. She tilted back her head and sang, "Holey, holey, holey!"

The story about Rachel is true. Rachel was beginning to recognize that there is a secret blanketed in the ordinary things of life.

Signs and Symbols

GOD HAS LOVED PEOPLE from the very beginning, and all God wants in return is love. But it is hard to love what you can't get your arms around. So, God became a human being in Jesus Christ. Catholics believe that in Christ, God shares divine life in many ways, but especially in the *sacraments*. In the sacraments, ordinary things reveal God. More than that, the sacraments *do* what they reveal. In the waters of Baptism, you die and rise with Christ. Eating and drinking at the Eucharist, you share in Christ's Body and Blood and his sacrifice on Calvary. In the laying on of hands at Confirmation, you share the coming of the Holy Spirit at Pentecost. Each sacrament is a joyful God-filled action in which Catholics celebrate their share in God's love.

1. *Initiation and welcome.* Christians belong together. The source of strength along the way comes from the loving support of others—the community of faith. Three sacraments welcome people to the way—Baptism, Confirmation, and Eucharist.

2. *Healing.* Reconciliation and healing mean much more than forgiveness and physical health. Reconciliation and healing are the Christian way of life. So there are two important sacraments of healing—Penance, or Reconciliation, for the forgiveness of sins and Anointing of the Sick for bringing the healing touch of Christ and the community's care to those who are ill.

3. *Ministry and vocation.* Baptism gives everybody a share in the priesthood of Christ, who welcomed, healed, and reconciled the world to God. As people on the way, the community cares for one another. The sacraments of Marriage and Holy Orders celebrate forms of ministry to the world and for the Church. Marriage celebrates the faithful, lasting love of a woman and a man in Christ. They commit themselves to serve God and each other. They promise to build up the human family. The love of married people is a sign of Christ's love for the Church.

The sacrament of Holy Orders celebrates the Church's strong commitment to leadership that enables all people on the way to live the Gospel, celebrate sacraments, witness to the Risen Lord, and serve one another. The Church ordains bishops, priests, and deacons to lead, encourage, challenge, and forgive everybody along the way.

The sacraments are reminders of Christ's love. They proclaim the presence of the Holy right in the middle of daily life. And the sacraments are reasons to make festival around all that is holy!

CELEBRATE THE HOLY

Where and how do you get a sense of the holy? Share some experiences.

2

A SENSE OF GRATITUDE

—

A Safety-Pin Corsage

NO MATTER WHAT GIFT Great-Aunt Emma ever got, she enjoyed every ribbon, every scrap of wrapping paper, every trinket. She would get just as excited about a gift of bath salts as she would over a diamond necklace.

Once, her grandniece Patty gave her an unidentifiable something-or-other made up of safety pins. Emma oohed and aahed over the thing. When Patty was unable to explain what the thingamabob was, Emma didn't bat an eye. She just popped open one of the pins and wore the thing all day long—as if it were a corsage. Great-Aunt Emma was thoughtful enough to really use the gifts she had been given.

Just before Great-Aunt Emma died, she planned her funeral. She was laid out in a simple black coffin. She had her beat-up, black rosary twined around her fingers. She wore her favorite flowered dress with the wide lapels. And there, right over her heart, was fastened the safety-pin corsage Patty had given her so many years before. It was still shiny, and it was going home with Emma—home to God.

Gracious, Grateful People

CHRISTIANS ARE (or should be) people like Great-Aunt Emma—gracious, grateful people. Sometimes you may not understand all your gifts. What is important is to accept your gifts, to try to use them, and to bring them with you to the end of the way—still shiny—home to God. This is a mark of gracious people—*eucharistic* people.

The Eucharist (the Mass) finds its roots in Jesus' Last Supper, death, and resurrection. Jesus chose a meal—a gathering of friends who shared a common life and love—to reveal God's love. Jesus' supper celebration had all the elements of a family meal and a festival. But Jesus did much more. Jesus took bread and wine and identified *himself* with them.

Celebrating Eucharist

WHETHER MASS IS CELEBRATED in a hut in the jungles of Nicaragua or in Saint Patrick's Cathedral in New York, whether it is hushed and hurried in a prison in the Ukraine or raises the roof for two hours in an African-American parish in Washington, D.C., it has the same simple elements.

1. Mass begins with a friendly greeting from the priest, and all mark themselves with the sign of their membership—in the name of the Father, and of the Son, and of the Holy Spirit.

2. The readings from Scripture are proclaimed. In particular, the Gospel helps the people join their stories to the story of Jesus. Everybody declares that this message is really good news.

3. Everybody joins his or her own personal gifts to the gift of Jesus, and all share in his sacrificial offering to God. In the Eucharistic Prayer, the priest prays the words spoken at the Last Supper. This meal is done *in memory* of Jesus. At the end of this great sacrificial prayer of remembering, voices are raised in praise and in a great *Amen*—so be it!

4. At Communion time, the members eat and drink the Body and Blood of Christ. At this special moment, the sharing of bread and wine which have become Jesus binds everyone more deeply to one another, to Christ, and to his great mission.

5. At the end of the Eucharist, everyone is sent away with a special commission—to go in peace to love and serve the Lord.

The Eucharist is part of the fabric of the faith. All the members bring their varied gifts to the Mass. And then they try—like Great-Aunt Emma—to live grateful and gracious lives *outside* the Eucharistic Celebration. Enjoy the Mass. Celebrate and use your gifts so that you will be able to bring them with you—still shiny—home to God.

LEARN GRATITUDE

How can you make Eucharist a regular part of your life?

3

A SENSE OF MEMORY

Built of Memories

SOMEONE ONCE ASKED an old lumberjack how long he'd had his ax. "Seventy years," the lumberjack said. "I've had to replace the steel head five times, and I've worn out twenty handles—all oak!"

The little you who looked in the mirror on your seventh birthday is the same you who looked in the mirror this morning and will look in the mirror thirty years from now. You are taller, your facial structure and body have changed, you have permanent teeth—and they may even be straight. And one day you will see gray hair and a few wrinkles. But it will be *you* doing the looking.

Everything you are comes to you from the past. You carry features and habits and gestures of ancestors you may never have heard of. Some are noticeable. Your eyes are dark brown or light blue, your hair is tightly curled or straight. You have yet to discover everything about you. You carry inside you centuries of history. Yet you are right here—a one-of-a-kind human person.

Catholic Memory

MEMORY IS VERY IMPORTANT to Catholics. That does not mean that Catholics live in the past. But the shared memories of the Church help you make decisions about today and plans for tomorrow.

Your Church memory reaches back to the beliefs, stories, and teachings of all God's People. Catholic memory is found in three important places.

1. *Sacred Scripture.* The stories and events that were spoken around campfires in the Mideast deserts and were handed down from generation to generation have been collected and written down in the Hebrew Scriptures, or Old Testament. The words, actions, and person of Jesus and the teaching of his early followers have been shared in the Christian Scriptures, or New Testament. For a member of the Church, this Bible is

more than a book or collection of books. It is God's Living Word. It is the very heart and soul of Church history.

2. *Church teaching.* From the very beginning, the faith community knew that the Scriptures alone were not enough. The gifts they had been given had to be lived out in time and space. They knew that the Scriptures had to be shared and put into practice. So, they put great stress on the ministry of *teaching.*

There are different kinds of teaching in the Catholic memory. One is *doctrine.* That is a word for the official teachings of the Church. This kind of teaching is handed down by popes and meetings of bishops. It is a very special and sacred memory. This memory ensures that all the members are remaining faithful to the Gospel of Jesus Christ. Another kind of teaching includes *customs and ritual.* A lot of Church teaching has to do with customs, or the way things are done, and with rituals, or the familiar repeated actions of liturgy.

3. *Lives well lived.* The Church's memory is also seen in the lives of people who have followed Jesus. Their faithfulness shows that the Gospel of Jesus can be lived and that it will make a difference in the world. That is why the Church has always made such a big fuss about saints and the times in which those saints lived.

There is a lot more to this sense of memory. You can't learn it all at once. Your Church will gradually reveal to you the wonders of its memory. People without memory miss the excitement of the present and have no future. Your Church with its rich memory can tackle the problems of today and can change and adapt to meet the future—always faithful to the Gospel.

KEEP THE MEMORY ALIVE

How can you keep the Church memory alive in you? (Remember Scripture, Church teaching, and lives well led.)

4

A SENSE OF
FORGIVENESS

The Two-Hanky Movie

CAMILLA LOVED OLD movies. There was no bigger treat than to spend a couple of hours at the Fine Arts Theater on Michigan Avenue or to rent a stack of cassettes and get lost in the black-and-white world of the 1930s and 40s.

"Oh, Johnny," moaned the dying heroine. "I forgive you, Johnny. I know you did me wrong! I know you were untrue. I know you sent the mob to kill my father. But lying here with this bullet in my heart, I still love you, and *(sigh)* I always will . . ." Her eyes close in death, the music swells, the screen darkens, and Camilla digs for her second hanky.

Called to Forgive

OF COURSE, THERE ARE other movies where people are not so forgiving. New heroes barge into the dens of evil with machine guns blazing—beating and killing everybody in sight.

For the People of God, forgiveness is not a heroic option or a sign of weakness. It is a way of life.

Evil is very, very real. That fact hasn't changed much since the days the Israelites were wandering in the desert. Moses had led the people out of slavery in Egypt, but they were still slaves to a lot of bad moral habits—a lot of sin. So, God made a covenant with the people.

> I, the Lord, am your God, who brought you out of the land of Egypt,
>   that place of slavery. You shall not have other gods besides me.
> You shall not take the name of the Lord, your God, in vain.
> Remember to keep holy the Sabbath day.
> Honor your father and your mother.
> You shall not kill.
> You shall not commit adultery.
> You shall not steal.

You shall not bear false witness against your neighbor.
You shall not covet your neighbor's spouse.
You shall not covet your neighbor's goods.

EXODUS 20:1, 7–8, 12–17

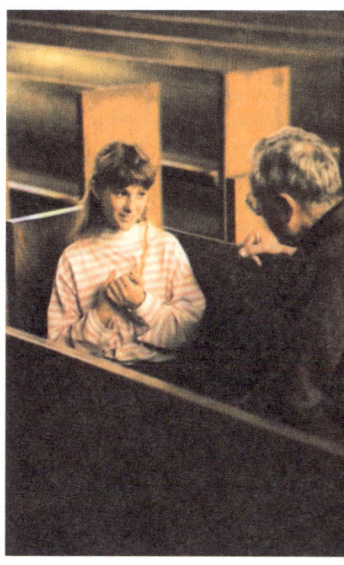

This covenant was on tablets of stone, but it was also written in the hearts of the people. They knew that they had a great Law to live by.

When Jesus came on the scene, he began giving a special gift to people—the gift of forgiveness. The Gospels are full of stories of Jesus forgiving.

When Jesus taught his followers to pray, he gave them the Lord's Prayer. The last words of that prayer are "forgive us our sins as we forgive those who sin against us." And Jesus, hanging as he was on a cross of shame, made one of his last living gasps words of forgiveness, "Father, forgive them, for they know not what they do."

Forgiveness is part of your very makeup as a follower of Jesus.

1. You belong to the community of the Church. Your belonging makes a difference to the community. The community does not want you to separate yourself by anger, by fear, or by sin.

2. You have the power to choose to do what is right. If, however, you choose to do what is wrong, you have set yourself against God and at odds with the community. This *is* sin.

3. If you are sorry for the wrong you have done, you can seek forgiveness. You can and must also *give* forgiveness.

4. The way you demonstrate your sorrow is by making your confession to a priest. In the Church, God's forgiveness is given by the priest, who acts in the person of Christ.

The community accepts all attempts at expressing and asking for forgiveness. The Church welcomes the sinner and provides a world in which the lost one can always come home and is made to feel as though he or she had never left.

FORGIVE ONE ANOTHER

What are some practical ways you can keep alive in you the sense of forgiveness?

5

A SENSE OF
SERVICE

—

A Project

THERE IS ANOTHER VERY special sense that Catholics share. That is the sense that people need one another—the sense that the best way to show that you follow Jesus Christ is to serve others. Service does not come naturally. So, as part of your Confirmation celebration, plan a project for yourself. You can do this service project by yourself or as part of a group. Use the space below to plan the project. Remember to make it very practical. Make it for a fixed period of time. Be sure to plan how you will evaluate the project after it is over.

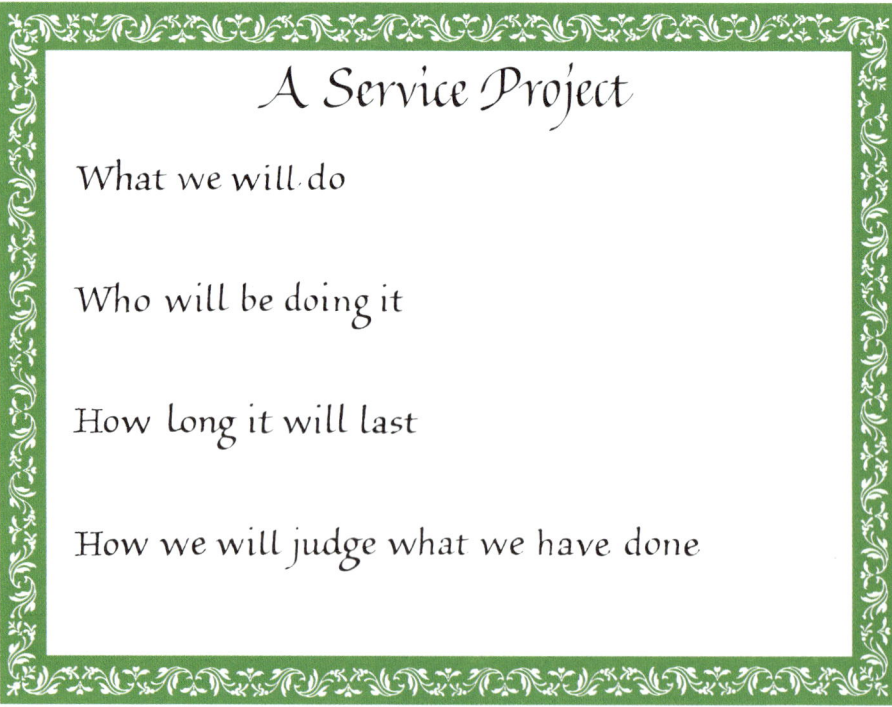

A Service Project

What we will do

Who will be doing it

How long it will last

How we will judge what we have done

Welcome to the Way!

Dear_____

You have received the invitation to join the community on the way of Jesus.

You have entered into a process of discovery and growth.

You have spent time searching for the gifts of the Holy Spirit:

    the gifts of wisdom and understanding,

    the gifts of judgment and courage,

    the gifts of knowledge and reverence,

    the gift of wonder and awe.

You are willing to accept full membership in the Church.

Come celebrate the sacrament of Confirmation with us

on_____
    (DAY AND DATE)

at_____
    (TIME)

in_____
    (PLACE)

with_____
    (BISHOP'S NAME)

                              Your friend,

                         _____
                         (PASTOR'S SIGNATURE)